PACK

W9-AHU-335

PJ GRAY

LIFESKILLS IN ACTION

LIVING SKILLS

MONEY

Living on a Budget | Road Trip
Opening a Bank Account | The Guitar
Managing Credit | High Cost
Using Coupons | Get the Deal
Planning to Save | Something Big

LIVING

Smart Grocery Shopping | Shop Smart
Doing Household Chores | Keep It Clean
Finding a Place to Live | A Place of Our Own
Moving In | Pack Up
Cooking Your Own Meals | Dinner Is Served

JOB

Preparing a Resume | Not Her Job
Finding a Job | Dream Jobs
Job Interview Basics | Job Ready
How to Act Right on the Job | Choices
Employee Rights | Not So Sweet

SADDLEBACK
EDUCATIONAL PUBLISHING
www.sdlback.com

All source images from Shutterstock.com

ISBN-13: 978-1-68021-042-2
ISBN-10: 1-68021-042-4
eBook: 978-1-63078-348-8

Printed in Malaysia

21 20 19 18 17   2 3 4 5 6

Grace and Hope are twins. They look alike. But they are very different people.

Grace is a planner. She is proud to be a nerd. Hope is not a planner. She does not like details. But she does like to have fun. Hope's motto is "Party first. Pay later."

Grace just finished college. And she has already found a new job. It is in another city. Her new boss wants her to move.

Hope stopped going to college. But she wants to return. Right now she works part-time.

The twins still live with their dad. Two weeks ago they all had dinner.

"I ordered it with bacon," their dad said.

"And lots of cheese?" Grace asked.

"Yes," he replied. "Just the way you like it."

They sat and talked about the move. Grace had just come back from the new city. She had found a new apartment there. It was a great deal, and it was big.

"Come with me," Grace said to Hope. "The

apartment has two bedrooms. It will be a fresh start for you. There is a school in that city."

"Okay," said Hope with a grin. "And I can help with the move."

"Oh," said Grace. "I don't know. I think I should handle it."

"Why?" Hope asked. "Don't you trust me?"

Grace said nothing. She looked at her dad.

"Fine!" Hope said. She left the room.

"Why did you do that?" their dad asked Grace.

"I did not want to hurt her."

"But you did."

"Hope is so bad with details," Grace said.

"She has to learn," their dad said. "You can help her. And you need the help. You will be working long hours. You can't do this alone. Do you want me to help?"

"No, Dad," Grace replied. "Thanks for asking, but we are adults."

"Then ask your sister for help," he replied. "It's her move too now."

Hope came back into the room.

"I need your help," Grace said. "Let's do this together."

Hope smiled. "Okay."

"We only have two weeks," Grace said. "And we have a lot to do!"

Grace asked Hope to find a moving company. "Make sure you get a good price. And get insurance!"

"Don't worry," Hope said.

"Can I make you a list?" Grace asked. "It will help you."

"No thanks," Hope replied. "I don't need one."

"Are you sure?" Grace asked.

Hope nodded. She wanted to say something but did not. She did not want to start a fight. Instead she said, "I will pack for us."

"Let me pack my own things," Grace replied. "You can pack our shared things."

Hope agreed.

The next day Hope looked for packing materials. She searched for a moving company.

Grace was also busy. She went to the post office. It was easy to fill out the change-of-address form. Then she gave their new address to the DMV. And to her bank and credit card company.

Grace planned the move-in date. Their new landlord agreed to the date. He gave her numbers to call for utilities. Grace had the electricity turned on. Then she called to get cable and Internet hooked up.

Soon the move was a week away. Grace was even busier. Her new job had started. She was staying with a friend during the week. The couch was not fun to sleep on. Grace could not wait to be in her new apartment.

Hope had quit her job to get ready for the move. Grace called her after work one day. "How is it going? Find a mover yet?"

"Yes!" Hope replied. "I got a great deal."

"Who are they?" Grace asked.

"Don't you trust me?"

"Yes, I do," Grace said.

"Good," Hope said. "Then don't worry. I found some boxes too. The grocery store had a bunch. They let me take some."

"Where are you now?" Grace asked.

"Getting my nails done," Hope said.

"Will you be home packing tonight?" Grace asked.

"No. My friends want to send me off with a party."

"Another one?"

"I have a lot of friends," Hope said.

That Friday, Grace texted Hope from her job. "I will be home tonight," she wrote. "Most of my things are packed. But I have a few clothes left."

"Okay," Hope replied.

"When are the movers coming?" Grace asked.

"Morning. Bright and early!"

"Good," Grace replied. She was still worried. Hope had never told her the name of the mover.

"Got to go," Hope wrote. "Must find more boxes."

The next morning Grace was up early. "Where are the movers?" she asked. "The drive will take three hours. And it will take time to load the truck."

"I called them," Hope said. "They will be here soon."

"We have to move today!" Grace said. "The weekend is my only time off. I told our new landlord we would move in today."

The movers arrived four hours later.

"You are late!" said Grace.

"This is the agreed upon time," the mover said.

"No, it's not!" Hope said. "You are late!" She looked at Grace. "I swear. It's not my fault."

"Did you get the start time in writing?" Grace asked.

Hope shook her head.

Grace was upset. "Just get the boxes into the van! They are over there."

The mover looked at all the boxes. "You will have to pay more," he said.

"Why?" Grace asked.

"That is a bigger load than we agreed upon."

Grace looked at Hope.

"I wanted to get the best deal," Hope said. "Who knew we would have this many boxes?"

Grace agreed to pay more. The movers began to pack the van.

"Some of these boxes will cost more," the mover said.

"Why?" Grace asked.

"They are too heavy."

Grace looked at Hope. "What did you do?"

"I ran out of boxes," Hope replied. "The big ones were all I had."

Grace agreed to pay more.

The movers took much longer than planned. Grace and Hope drove ahead to the new city. They got the keys from the landlord. Then they waited for the movers.

"What is taking them so long?" Grace asked.

"Calm down!" Hope said.

"Calm down?" Grace asked. "Why should I?"

"Go ahead," Hope replied. "Tell me it's all my fault. You always do!"

"Just call them back again! Find out where they are."

"I keep getting their voice mail."

The sun set. It was dark outside. The movers arrived late. Very late.

"What took you so long?" Grace asked the driver.

"We got a flat tire," he replied. "Then we got a little lost."

Grace was mad.

The mover looked around. "So your apartment is on the second floor?" he asked.

"Yes," Grace said. "Why?"

"It will cost you another fee," he said.

"Are you joking?"

"No," he said. "Having to go up and down stairs costs more."

"Just put the boxes by the curb," said Grace. "We will do the rest."

"Hope!" Grace called out. "Get over here! Help me get our things into the apartment."

"Wait," Hope said. "They do that."

"Only if we pay more," Grace replied.

Grace was mad. And tired. She and Hope began to take things up to the apartment. Hope picked up a box. They both heard a sound. It sounded like broken glass.

"Did you buy moving insurance?" Grace asked.

Hope shook her head.

Grace looked at the items on the sidewalk. A bookcase was broken. So was a chair.

The movers finished unloading the van. The driver smiled at Grace. He held out his hand. Grace just looked at him.

"No tip?" he asked.

"Here is a tip," Grace replied. "If you see me again, run for your life."

They watched the van drive away. It had been a very long day. Now it was late. Grace was hot and tired. Her back hurt. All she wanted was a shower.

Grace looked at all of the boxes. There were boxes stacked in the living room. More boxes were in the kitchen. There were even boxes on tables and chairs. None of them were marked.

"Hope!" Grace called out.

Hope was on her cell phone. "Hang on!" she replied.

"Where are the bath towels?" Grace asked. "Where is the soap? Where is anything?"

Hope shook her head. "I forgot to mark the boxes."

Grace sighed. She opened a box. Hope watched her. There were drinking glasses and dinner plates inside. Some were broken.

Grace found a bath towel. Hope had used towels to wrap the plates.

"I did not want them to break," Hope said softly.

The doorbell rang. "What now?" Grace said loudly. "That better not be a mover coming back!"

Hope went to the front door and returned. Grace looked up. Hope was holding a pizza box.

"I called ahead," Hope said. "When you were not looking."

Grace smiled.

"It's just how you like it," Hope said. "Bacon with lots of cheese."

What mistakes did Grace and Hope make in planning their move? Want to learn more about how to move smart? Just flip the book!

JUST *flip* THE BOOK!

Moving to a new place is exciting.

But it is a lot of work too.

A move takes planning.

You have to pack.

Get the boxes to your new place.

And unpack.

It can take weeks.

How will you do it all?

Go step by step.

First make a list of jobs.

Complete them one by one.

Try to do a few jobs each week.

Use a calendar.

Mark the day you will move.

Plan to get all jobs done by then.

6

14

Pack up
bedroom

13

2

10

9

Buy boxes
and tape

17

16

Move in!

15

23

22

30

29

5

Next decide who will do the moving.

You can hire a company.

A **mover** makes things easy.

Workers do the hard part.

They lift and load boxes.

And move the heavy things.

But hiring a mover costs money.

It can cost a lot.

Many people do their own moving.

They pack the boxes.

And drive them to their new place.

This takes more time.

But the cost is much less.

Having a pickup helps.

It is a great way to move a few boxes.

What if you have more?

Think about **renting** a moving truck.

These come in many sizes.

Get one that will hold all your things.

Call several truck companies.

Look for the best deal.

Ask about other ways to save.

Some days during the week
may cost less.

Are you a student?

Have you served in the military?

Ask about **discounts**.

$29/hour

Studer
Receiv

25

You will need to **reserve** the rental truck.

Do this online or by phone.

The company will want your license number.

They may want to know your age.

You will have to pay a **deposit**.

This will hold the truck.

You can get the money back.

Just return the truck in good shape.

Accidents can happen.

The truck may get a dent.

You will have to pay for this.

Check your **insurance** to be safe.

Call your insurance company.

Find out if a rental truck is covered.

If not, get insurance from the rental company.

They give you many choices.

Don't pay more than you have to.

Get just what you need.

There is more to do before you move.

Utilities have to be hooked up.

Some may come with your new place.

Water and trash often do.

Call to get others set up.

Electricity. Gas. Internet. TV.

Do it a week or two before you move.

It can take days to set up a new service.

Think about phone service.

You may have a cell phone.

But do you want a **landline** too?

Some people do just to be safe.

A cell phone can break.

It can get lost or stolen.

A landline can be worth the cost.

Decide if it is right for you.

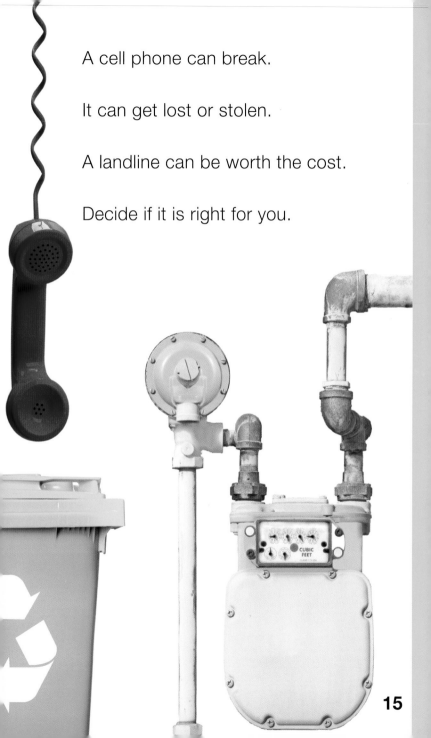

Packing takes a lot of time.

Being organized helps.

It makes unpacking much easier.

First get the **supplies** you need.

Boxes. Packing paper.

Moving blankets. Tape.

The truck rental company sells supplies.

But they can be costly.

There are ways to save.

Get free boxes from local stores.

Use old newspapers to wrap items.

Pack with your own blankets or rugs.

Use T-shirts and towels too.

Buy things at a discount store.

Tape. Markers. Labels.

Fragile

Kitchen

Living Room

Bedroom

Pack by room.

Do not put too many items in a box.

Make sure you can lift it.

Put heavy items in small boxes.

Light items can go in bigger boxes.

Some items break easily.

Plates. Mugs. Photo frames.

They are **fragile**.

Wrap them with paper.

Put blankets and towels around them.

Write the word *fragile* on the box.

Some items get used every day.

An alarm clock. Medicine.

Sheets and towels.

Set aside a box for these things.

Pack them on the day of the move.

Label the box so you can find it.

Unpack First

Plan to **change your address**.

Do this two weeks before the move.

Go to the post office. Fill out a form.

The form is online too.

Make a list of who sends you mail.

Banks. Credit card companies.

Insurance. DMV.

Your job or school.

Let them know your new address.

It's the day of the move.

Make sure you have help.

Load big items first.

Start with furniture and heavy boxes.

Put boxes with fragile items in last.

You may want to take these in your car.

Your new place may look empty.

But all the boxes will quickly fill it up.

Be organized as you unload.

Unpacking takes time.

It won't get done all at once.

Start with the rooms you use most.

Kitchen. Bathroom. Bedroom.

Do a little each day.

You may need some new items.

Furniture.

Silverware.

A vacuum.

Ask your family before buying new things.

They may have old items to give you.

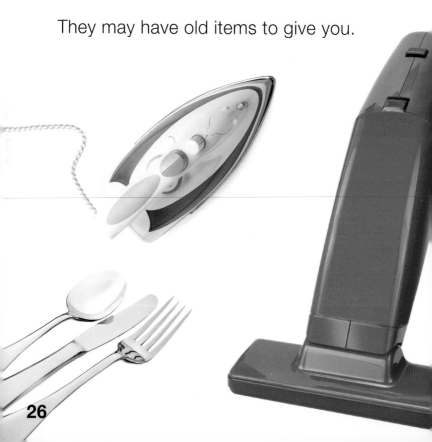

Save money by shopping at **thrift stores**.

Go to yard sales.

Look online for things people are selling.

Used items can work just as well as new ones.

And they cost a lot less.

Check them before you buy them.

Make sure they work.

Some furniture stores offer deals.

They may be going out of business.

Or need to make room for new items.

They may have damaged items.

A table with a small scratch.

Or a sofa with a tiny tear.

These are often marked down a lot.

Take a look.

You will need cleaning supplies.

And items to keep them in.

A laundry basket. Plastic bins.

A broom and a mop.

It's all part of having your own place.

Moving is hard work.

There are many jobs to do.

Rent a truck.

Set up utilities.

Pack and unpack.

But the hard work is worth it.

At last you have your own place.

Enjoy it!

What can go wrong with a move? That is what Grace and Hope find out in *Pack Up*. Want to read on?

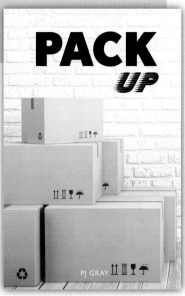

JUST *flip* THE BOOK!